WHERE EPICS FAIL

WHERE EPICS FAIL

Meditations to Live By

YAHIA LABABIDI

Unbound

This edition first published in 2018

Unbound

6th Floor Mutual House,
70 Conduit Street, London W1S 2GF

www.unbound.com

Text design by Patty Rennie

A CIP record for this book is available
from the British Library

ISBN 978-1-78352-582-9 (trade paperback)
ISBN 978-1-78352-583-6 (ebook)
ISBN 978-1-78352-581-2 (limited edition)

Printed in Great Britain by CPI Group (UK)

A special thank you to Miguel Fernandez and Rakia Maher for their support of this book

Dear Reader,

The book you are holding came about in a rather different way to most others. It was funded directly by readers through a new website: Unbound. Unbound is the creation of three writers. We started the company because we believed there had to be a better deal for both writers and readers. On the Unbound website, authors share the ideas for the books they want to write directly with readers. If enough of you support the book by pledging for it in advance, we produce a beautifully bound special subscribers' edition and distribute a regular edition and ebook wherever books are sold, in shops and online.

This new way of publishing is actually a very old idea (Samuel Johnson funded his dictionary this way). We're just using the internet to build each writer a network of patrons. At the back of this book, you'll find the names of all the people who made it happen.

Publishing in this way means readers are no longer just passive consumers of the books they buy, and authors are free to write the books they really want. They get a much fairer return too – half the profits their books generate, rather than a tiny percentage of the cover price.

If you're not yet a subscriber, we hope that you'll want to join our publishing revolution and have your name listed in one of our books in the future. To get you started, here is a £5 discount on your first pledge. Just visit unbound.com, make your pledge and type **EPIC5** in the promo code box when you check out.

Thank you for your support,

Dan, Justin and John
Founders, Unbound

This book is dedicated to all mystics—especially Sufis—whose art of living is a soure of sustenance and inspiration, on the page as well as off

Epigrams succeed where epics fail.

PERSIAN PROVERB

Ah, to be one of them! One of the poets whose song helps close the wound rather than open it!

JUAN RAMÓN JIMÉNEZ

FOREWORD

An Atlas of Tiny Maps: On Reading Yahia Lababidi's Aphorisms

DR MATHEW STAUNTON

It is unlikely that this is your first encounter with aphorisms. You have surely heard them quoted and read them both in isolation and embedded in other texts. Like me, though, you may have come to this book with lingering doubts about what makes an aphorism an aphorism and how we distinguish one from, say, a proverb or an axiom. Aphorisms are popular. Discussions about what they are and how they work are much less so. A survey of the introductions to collections and anthologies reveals a mess of barely helpful definitions, all of which proclaim little more than that aphorisms are short and express some sort of general truth.

That they are short/pithy/concise is indisputable. This is one of the strengths of the aphorism: it can be easily memorized, recalled at will, or slipped into conversations, essays, and messages. The second criterion is more problematic. Consider this definition by W. H. Auden and Louis Kronenberger from the introduction to their *Viking*

Book of Aphorisms (1962): "An aphorism ... must convince every reader that it is either universally true or true of every member of the class to which it refers, irrespective of the reader's convictions."[*]

The notion that there was such a thing as "universal truth" was still acceptable in the 1960s but is viewed today with widespread skepticism. In a twenty-first century that has seen even heliocentrism denied,[†] it makes little sense to continue to judge aphorisms by this liquid yardstick when we can focus on other, more solid characteristics. This is the approach favored by James Geary, a prolific and very insightful commentator on aphoristic writing. His "Five Laws of the Aphorism" do not include truth:

1. It must be brief.
2. It must be personal.
3. It must be definitive.
4. It must be philosophical.
5. It must have a twist.[‡]

---

[*] W. H. Auden and Louis Kronenberger, *The Viking Book of Aphorisms*, New York: Dorset Press, 1981 (first edition 1962), p. vii.
[†] See, for example, Marshall Hall's astonishing book *The Earth is not Moving*, Fair Education Foundation, 1991, or any of the articles on www.fixedearth.com.
[‡] James Geary, "What are Geary's five laws of the aphorism?" in Frequently Unasked Questions, *All Aphorisms, All the Time*, www.jamesgeary.com/fuq.php?PHPSESSID=c90cb6020cc4-foead618c0c21cd94a39. Retrieved 5 January 2015.

Geary recognizes that the assertiveness and authoritativeness of the aphorist are more important than the perceived veracity of the aphorism itself. The statement must be definitive rather than true. Laws four and five suggest that aphorisms can also be considerably more exciting than Auden and Kronenberger's dusty definition would have us believe. Aphorisms are expressions of the profound critical thinking and literary prowess of their authors. They must be well crafted and thought-provoking.

Hippocrates (460–370 BC), the "Father of Medicine" and progenitor of all modern aphorists, would not pass Geary's test. Here is one of his aphorisms: "The spring is frequently attended with mania, melancholia, epilepsy, hemorrhage, angina, defiuxions of the head, hoarseness, cough, leprosy, cutaneous affections, white leprosy, ulcerative pustules, tubercles, and arthritic pains."[*]

Despite being brief, pedagogical, memorizable, and very definitely the distillation of considerable experience and expertise, this nugget of medical knowledge does not satisfy modern anthologists and critics. Hippocrates, we are told, used his aphorisms "not to spin general truths but to record precise, factual details."[†] The astute

---

[*] Elias Marks (ed.), *The Aphorisms of Hippocrates*, New York: Collins and Co., 1817, p. 67.

[†] Hannah Brooks-Motl, "The smallest space: lyric aphorism in contemporary poetry" in *The Kenyon Review Online*, Spring 2013, www.kenyonreview.org/kr-online-issue/2013-spring/selections/hannah-brooks-motl-656342. Retrieved 5 January 2015.

observation we expect from a good aphorism is present here, but those readers who are looking for stimulating philosophy will be disappointed.

Law number two is just as crucial as the other four. What distinguishes the aphorism from its almost identical sibling, the proverb, is the fact that the former has an individual author and we know who that author is: Nietzsche, Mae West, Mark Twain, Jane Austen, Ralph Waldo Emerson, Goethe, Paul Valéry, Kafka and other well-known literati or people of experience and wisdom. There is no disguising the fact that women are massively under-represented in this field. Only 5 percent of the authors presented in *The Viking Book of Aphorisms* are women. The figure is similar in Geary's *Guide to the World's Great Aphorists*. Geary presents various theories but struggles to find an explanation for this anomaly:

> In researching my books, I was acutely aware of the preponderance of male aphorists. But I couldn't come up with a satisfactory explanation for it. The obvious explanation is: For centuries women were discouraged from pursuing literary careers, or any careers at all, so that's why there are fewer female aphorists.[*]

---

[*] James Geary, "Why are there fewer female than male aphorists?" on *All Aphorisms, All the Time*, August 2010. www.jamesgeary.com/blog/why-are-there-fewer-female-than-male-aphorists. Retrieved 5 January 2015.

He suggests that evolutionary biology and psychology might offer further explanation but does not improve on his initial hypothesis. One of his readers has pointed out that "when a woman is an aphorist, they call her a mother."[*] That a mother is considered wise is evidenced by the fact that in France if a woman has three or more children, she can sit the civil service exam to become a primary school teacher without having done any studies beforehand. Outside of this role, however, there have been few acceptable outlets for this wisdom until relatively recently, and as the nineteenth-century French historian Jules Michelet has taught us, in darker times overstepping societal limits could land a woman in the dunking chair.[†]

The authoritativeness of the aphorist, be they male or female, can still rankle. Susan Sontag, as well as Auden and Kronenberger, reacts to the position of superiority adopted by the aphorist with various degrees of suspicion. All three describe aphoristic writing as the product of "aristocratic thinking."[‡] "To write aphorism is"—according to Sontag—"to assume a mask—a mask of scorn, of superiority."[§] The philosopher Jacques Derrida,

---

* Anonymous, cited by James Geary, *ibid*.
† See Jules Michelet's *La Sorcière*, Paris: Garnier-Flammarion, 1966.
‡ Auden and Kronenberger, *op. cit*., p. vii; Susan Sontag, *As Consciousness is Harnessed to Flesh: Diaries 1964–1980*, Harmondsworth: Penguin Books, 2013, p. 521.
§ Sontag, *ibid*.

too, perceives that the relationship between the aphorist and his/her reader is not one of equals:

> Aphorism can, of course, turn out to be a device of rhetoric, a sly calculation aiming at the greatest authority, an economy or strategy of mastery which knows very well how to potentialize meaning ("see how I formalize, in so few words I always say more than would appear").[*]

This superiority is, however, a part of the process. We do not leaf through a collection of aphorisms to have somebody like us simply confirm our beliefs. We look to a person who claims to be wiser than us to present us with something new and provocative. The aristocratic position of the aphorist is not unlike the "good breeding" described by Mark Twain in one of his aphorisms: "Good breeding consists of concealing how much we think of ourselves and how little we think of the other person."[†]

The aphorism is both the product and the sign of this aristocracy. The mask of the aristocrat (including literary aristocrats like Auden and Sontag) is the self-confident mask of the doctor for whose patients doubt or hesitation would be counterproductive.

---

[*] Jacques Derrida in Derek Attridge (ed.), *Acts in Literature*, New York: Routledge, 1992, p. 417.
[†] Albert Bigelow Paine (ed.), *Mark Twain's Notebooks*, New York: Harper and Brothers, 1935, p. 345.

You are here

Derrida glosses the word "aphorism" with characteristic efficiency (and no shortage of aristocratic thinking): "As its name indicates, aphorism separates, it marks dissociation (*apo*), it terminates, delimits, arrests (*horizō*). It brings to an end by separating, it separates in order to end—and to define (*finir—et définir*)."[*]

It divides the totality of existence into a series of manageable chunks. Happily, this lets Hippocrates back in. The primary service provided by the aphorist is one of guidance. To those of us who find ourselves lost in a mystifying, bewildering, and potentially terrifying morass of data, the aphorist provides a signpost/landmark that briefly reduces/distills multiple choices/interpretations/ pathways to one before leaving us to our own devices. Cutting through the panic-inducing relativism of competing perspectives with the minimalist products of his/her reflections, the aphorist provides us with a moment of clarity. The aphorism is, thus, a tool to help us on our way rather than our final destination. What we do with that moment, how we use these interpretations and signposts is up to us. James Geary gives us a rare insight into how his process works:

> That's the point of [an anthology of aphorisms]: to
> be a Swiss army knife for the mind. For more than

---

[*] Derrida, *op. cit.*, p. 416.

thirty-five years now, I've carried a small stock of aphorisms around in my head. When I was laid off, a blade with one of Vilhelm Ekelund's sharpest sayings flashed out. That aphorism didn't solve any of my problems, of course. But it did help me cut through the chaos of the moment to see a place where I could make a stand. Consult this set of sayings in emergencies of the head, heart, or hands.*

Aphorisms invite us to reflect on our own position through the prism of a wiser person's vision, and plot our next move. It is as if we were wandering confused in a city and came across a map with friendly, readable typefaces, a carefully researched color palette and, most importantly, a soothing message, printed in bold and circled to leave us in no doubt: **You Are Here**. The aphorism is as authoritative as a signpost. Somebody who knows the best way to the New York Public Library has indicated an efficient route. What you do with this information is your own business.

This analogy with navigation and mapping is worth developing. The potential for panic in the built environment was addressed by Kevin Lynch in his groundbreaking study of user-friendly urban design, *The Image of the City* (1960). Lynch mentions terror only once at the beginning of his manifesto, but it is a reference that informs and resonates through the rest of the book:

---

* James Geary, *Geary's Guide to the World's Great Aphorists*, New York: Bloomsbury Publishing, 2007, p. 3.

> To become completely lost is perhaps a rather rare experience for most people in the modern city ... But let the mishap of disorientation once occur, and the sense of anxiety and even terror that accompanies it reveals to us how closely it is linked to our sense of balance and well-being. The very word "lost" in our language means much more than simple geographical uncertainty; it carries overtones of utter disaster.[*]

While writing *The Image of the City* Lynch did not believe that people lost their way in cities very often. He was clearly thinking of an American individual navigating his/her way through a city filled with signage in English and opportunities to ask passers-by for assistance. But if we place the same person in a modern megacity with signage in non-Latin alphabets, spaghetti-like public transport networks, uninterpretable visual cues, and nobody (s)he can communicate with, we have no difficulty in imagining the potential for getting lost. Lynch did not anticipate the scale of this potential as it is now, more than half a century after he published his book, but was, nonetheless, unequivocal about the unfortunate impact of such a predicament.

---

[*] Kevin Lynch, *The Image of the City*, Cambridge: MIT Press, 1960, p. 4.

Reality is a rose of a thousand petals

A collection of Yahia Lababidi's aphorisms is, therefore, like an atlas of tiny maps, each one guiding us calmly through a network of possibilities to a bright and often unexpected vista. Gem-like, they are, as he says himself, the "marriage of heaven and hell: poetry and philosophy," and frequently resemble haiku. Consider this one: "Branches are roots, too, in the sky." There is something essential here: the delightful epiphany that opens the mind of the reader to an awareness of the natural world and its link to human nature. The personal "I" is known— we know it's Lababidi—but is absent from the statement. This is a speakerless text, almost wordless. Silence and the banishing of the monkey mind that characterizes haiku and Buddhism is foregrounded. As he writes himself, "Aphorisms respect the wisdom of silence by disturbing it, briefly."

Nonetheless, aphorisms are not haiku: "A haiku is impressionistic, imagistic, leaving an emotion or feeling rather than a thought in its wake. An aphorism, while often deploying startling imagery, always provokes thought in addition to emotion and feeling."[*]

In his aphorisms, Lababidi is in full declarative mode. He does not argue, explain, or suggest. He asserts. He is

---

[*] James Geary, "What is the difference between an aphorism and a haiku?" in *All Aphorisms, All the Time*, www.jamesgeary.com/fuq.php. Retrieved 5 January 2015.

didactic but does not do our thinking for us. He provides us with his insights (shining a light, untangling the spaghetti, unfolding a map) and then encourages us to think for ourselves. As with all collections of aphorisms, each individual text is a whole in itself rather than a fragment of a whole. Lababidi playfully jumps from subject to subject, from reflection to reflection, sometimes dwelling on an idea through several aphorisms before moving into new territory. As we progress through the book we are confronted with his thinking on silence, pain, forgiveness, vice, debauchery, meditation, love . . . sometimes subjects we neither expect nor feel we need to consider. But, once read, we do consider them.

Before I began my journey through Lababidi's universe, I had no idea that I needed to think about forgiveness and not just think about it for a moment and then get back to my projects and preoccupations, but to really think about it. And yet, the following aphorism has been in my mind for months. I have repeated it to friends and students, in person and via social media: "Forgive them; damaged people can hardly imagine the pain they inflict on others." Of all the tiny maps in this collection, this is the one that has been giving me the most guidance. It begs questions (Who should I forgive? Who have I hurt?) while offering a definitive course of action (forgive them).

Currently, Lababidi's aphorism is the starting point for much of my own thinking on forgiveness and pain, just as a line from Samuel Beckett's short story *"Sans"* lurks in the background when I think about perseverance and hope: "*Pleuvra sur lui comme au temps béni du bleu la nuée passagère*" (On him will rain again as in the blessed days of blue, the passing cloud).[*]

These words bring me comfort and the tools I need to begin to move forward when I am close to abandoning a project. They are not the solution to my problem but the means to finding my own solution. Lababidi's texts are short and quickly read, but they continue in the mind of the reader after the page has been turned and the book is closed. It is as American literary critic George Steiner writes in *Language and Silence*: "When the word of the poet ceases, a great light begins."[†]

DR MATHEW STAUNTON is an Irish book
historian, prize-winning poetry publisher,
and teacher working between Paris and Oxford.

---

[*] Samuel Beckett, "*Sans*" in *Têtes-Mortes*, Paris: Les Éditions de Minuit, 1972, p. 70.
[†] George Steiner, *Language and Silence*, London: Faber and Faber, 2010 (first edition 1958), p. 58.

INTRODUCTION

Pearls and Provocation: The Mystic Humanism of Yahia Lababidi

KRIS SAKNUSSEMM

My great-grandfather on my father's side was one of the most famous American evangelists of his day. He was a key figure in the Baptist Society's Chapel Rail Car ministry (his personal train carriage was The Evangeline), which traveled the American hinterlands, spreading the Gospel as much like mustard seeds on the wind as he could. He was also one of the first men to ever play baseball for money. From the northern woods of Minnesota to the shipping yards of Mobile, he often used baseball, on his hymn-singing whistle-stops, as a means of bringing people together and encouraging them to attend services.

Something of this curious oscillation between the secular and the sacred persisted in my father, who was a Congregationalist minister. He graduated at the top of his class from the Pacific School of Religion in Berkeley, and had a profound devotion to theology. I spent hours as a child on the floor of his library as he prepared his sermons. Above my head, and certainly over my head then, was a treasure trove of religious longing. When I could still only appreciate and assimilate the smell of the books, I knew I was in the presence of something important: every single edition of the Bible in English at the time; complex explanations of Protestantism versus Catholicism; important works on Islam, Judaism, Hinduism, and Buddhism. From the Scholastics to Sufism, the names and ideas swirled around me like leaves in the sun: Meister Eckhart, Kierkegaard, Bonhoeffer, Tillich, May.

Whenever my father hit an impasse in his sermon writing, he would pause at his desk to hand-tie one of his gorgeously intricate fishing flies as a kind of practical, earthly way to clear his mind. Even as a child, I intuitively understood that he was torn between the personal sense of search his books embodied, and the desire to reach people from the pulpit and to change lives through face-to-face pastoral counseling. One of his hands turned pages, the other performed baptisms. He had one leg in a trout stream of secret, mystical hope and inquiry—and the other hustling up a pancake breakfast for the homeless. For him, there were many mysteries within the Christian tradition, but the single greatest personal conflict was between James and Paul. James says that faith without works is dead—yet Paul writes in Ephesians, "For by grace are ye saved through faith, and that not of yourselves—it is the gift of God—not of works lest any man should boast." It is hard to get more contrary than that.

More so than any book I have read in a long time—outside of any one religious tradition—the one you are holding has reinvigorated these moments and questions for me, and helped me reconcile them.

I first discovered the writing of Yahia Lababidi when some of his aphorisms were published alongside mine in an issue of a literary journal called *Hotel Amerika*. I have always been intrigued by the special challenge and power of the aphorism. It may well be regarded as one of the oldest literary forms, and yet, in this age of Facebook memes, text messages, and sound bites, it could still be the most accessible and relevant form of literary expression there is. Reading Lababidi's, I felt that rare exhilaration of meeting a kindred spirit. Since then, we have had many communications—from grand debates on the nature and significance of religion today, to ethical and moral issues in world politics, to the prickly matter of the role of the artist, stretched between being a lone explorer (a stranger and pilgrim), and a highly socialized being, seeking connection and communion with others.

Listen to his rhythm and symmetry . . . "We are born with one umbilical cord but die with many." I used to dive for black pearls in the Indian Ocean. I value this pearl of great price of his more than I can say.

Is it important that Lababidi is an Egyptian-American? I believe it absolutely is. The Egyptians I have had the pleasure to know are some of the warmest, most hospitable, and gregarious people I have ever met. They are also deeply respectful of silences. Think of the swarming, chaotic streets and lanes of Cairo, and then the stillness of the desert. This part of the world is one of the crucial origin points of myth, magic, and monotheism, and these many crossroads converge in Lababidi's thought poetry, which has the heart and sincerity to risk rising to wisdom—while always welcoming you to participate.

To compare Lababidi to Confucius, Heraclitus, and Augustine is stepping into a big, ever-changing river—which is exactly what my father the fisherman, and a Fisher of Men, would recommend. I find Lababidi's aphorisms confronting and inviting, in the great tradition of Novalis and Pascal. I also think of the wonderfully human-fragile Alan Watts, whom I once met as a child. In my own spiritual/social conflicts of inquiry, I go back to Watts, and to William James. And I go back to the work you have in hand right now.

Are Lababidi's pearls and provocations didactic? I find them deeply inclusive and validating of my very private questions—and that word that hides within questions: quest. At a time in history when secularism and the heritage power of the great world religions are more at odds than perhaps ever before, I find this artist's search into the meaning of faith and the faith in meaning like unto St. Veronica's wiping of a certain face. If there is a contemporary writer of blood and time who is seeking to bridge the peculiar gap between the mystic and the socialized human, it is Yahia Lababidi. Read him and you will find water you can hold in your hand, wind you can see.

KRIS SAKNUSSEMM is the author of
eleven books, including *Zanesville*.

4

APHORISMS

A poem arrives like a hand in the dark.

＊

A poem should be flesh-warm, scented spirit.

＊

Poems are like bodies; a fraction of their power resides
in their skin. The rest belongs to the spirit that swims
through them.

＊

Words seldom stand alone; like us, they are encircled
by the spirits of ancestors.

There's nothing casual about intimacy, or passing through a temple without bowing.

*

Where ocean and shore greet, a metaphor for where spirit and body meet.

*

The spirit cautions: beware of surrendering to the body or mind.

*

An unfree body cannot house a free spirit.

Body: a haunted echo chamber.

*

Exhibitionist: one who conceals depths through
revealing surfaces.

*

Strange, that surfaces should be celebrated,
yet depths apologized for.

*

Chance is what we call our failure to understand.

One must be careful to keep their balance when they carry a whole world inside of them.

*

Every enmity with another is part of our unfinished work; a free person has no enemies.

*

We are responsible for our enemy. Compassion is to consider the role we play in their creation.

*

Part of the inescapable truth of our interconnectedness is that compassion for the suffering of others lessens our own.

The only real borders are those of our compassion.

*

We can lend ideas our breath, but ideals require
our entire lives.

*

All who are tormented by an ideal must learn to make
an ally of failure.

*

The hungry and sated regard food and temptation
differently.

Hedonism, mistrustful of life's bounty, is left with a fistful of feathers (while the Great Beauty flies away).

✳

Pleasure might be snatched from life's hands; but joy, like all blessings, must be granted.

✳

And when we think we are stealing from life's fleeting pleasures, we are stealing from our own eternal joy.

✳

To stand a chance, we must give up what we desire most.

The ascetic does not deny pleasure; he shuns what is coarse in favor of the refined and exalted.

✳

There is a hidden relation between sacrifice and revelation—we are favored in proportion to what we are able to offer up.

✳

The ascetic ideal speaks thus: indulge, and forego vision.

✳

Psychedelics might offer visionary glimpses, but we're afforded more potent and enduring vision pursuing a life of patient virtue.

A virtuous man's good deeds are revealed, posthumously.

*

There are no shortcuts to transcendence.

*

Don't squander your boredom; dig deeper, treasures
are buried there.

*

The limits of our vision determine the limits of our
world.

One can't be too dismissive of the puppet show,
so long as they have strings attached.

✳

All languages are rough translations of our native
tongue: spirit.

✳

The path of the spirit: initiation into subtleties
upon subtleties.

✳

The world of images is not that of the spirit.

Poetic ideal: a language scrubbed clean by silences.

*

Some silences are more damning than words;
they are actions.

*

Certain silences are hard to take back with words.

*

When it comes to silence, there's boldness to shyness.

The poet's responsibility to society? Spiritual hygiene.

*

The worst type of ostentation is spiritual.

*

Spiritual fast food leads to spiritual indigestion.

*

Silence is the great jeweler of words—certifying their authenticity and assessing their true worth.

Aphorisms respect the wisdom of silence by disturbing it, briefly.

✳

Of all that is spoken, trust best what silence whispers.

✳

The air is dense with stray spirits, swarming for soul.

✳

Poem: an especially fine net for catching elusive states.

As protection from your lower soul, surround yourself with reminders of your higher soul.

✳

The divided self is still spiritually immature. Divine union begins with self-unity.

✳

Said a poem to a poet: Can I trust you? Is your heart pure to carry me? Are your hands clean to pass me on?

✳

For the sake of a good line, a poet, like a comedian, must be willing to risk everything.

From what you have, create what you have not.
The poem teaches the poet.

*

An engagement with the Divine can only be broken off
at the risk of spiritual death.

*

An apocalyptic viewpoint is a veiled death wish.
Perhaps wishing is the first part of willing.

Nietzsche's concept of Superman only makes sense,
spiritually, as one who self-overcomes.

✳

Numbness is a spiritual malady; true detachment
its remedy.

✳

The antidote to numbness is to care for
something . . . anything.

✳

We return revitalized from exalted regions of the soul,
stirred by art or spirituality, and with renewed care
for one another.

There is poetry for every region of the soul.

*

Lived poetry is practiced tenderness.

*

The contemplative life is not a passive one.

*

Poetry is the distance between us and our pain.

You can't bury pain and not expect it to grow roots.

✳

The one who hates themself sees that hated self in everyone they meet.

✳

Uncontrolled, self-loathing can consume the world.

✳

If we care for ourselves, we may turn our pain into gifts for others.

If we do not care for our souls, we become a burden for others.

*

Caring for our soul is the first step in caring for the world soul.

*

As we make peace with ourselves, we become more tolerant of our faults—in others.

*

Cruelty is hereditary—with nations, too.

Forgive them; damaged people can hardly imagine the pain they inflict on others.

✴

If there is someone we might ask forgiveness of, then there is no one we can deny forgiveness to.

✴

When we pass, perhaps we are pardoned only if we are forgiven by all whom we wronged.

✴

If we can try to see the (oftentimes, hurt) child in others, we are more likely to forgive them.

Spiritually speaking, what applied to us as children remains true as adults; we may only play once we've completed our homework.

✳

A child refusing to bathe, and preferring to play in mud, is not unlike an adult avoiding a cleansing encounter with the Spirit.

✳

Childhood imagination exercises, such as cloud-gazing, might become spiritual disciplines if carried over into adulthood.

✳

Work without the need for a vacation is a vocation.

If we accept art as a facet of the Divine, we better appreciate the gulf between the monument of the work and the wreck that is the worker.

*

To bridge the gulf between art and artist; this is the spiritual work.

*

Emotional neediness repels because of the expectation that others must do the hard work of the self for us.

*

They are not virtues if we are overly aware of them.

Unchecked insecurities become vices.

✻

Vice does not require a wide-open door to enter—just a crack will do.

✻

Demonic possession does not occur overnight; it requires a steadily weakened spiritual immune system.

✻

Sometimes the source of our power is a vice, harnessed.

Our vices make a hell of solitude, our virtues a heaven.

*

Debauchery, eventually, ushers in virtue. But there are less violent paths, such as patience.

*

Patience is not just waiting; it's also doing while we wait.

*

One distinction between diabolical and Divine inspiration is the duration of pleasure it affords.

To shield yourself against the evils of this world, keep your lips wet with the taste of revelation.

*

The unmet promises we make—to ourselves and others—return to taunt us.

*

To accept revelation, and the promise of new life, we must be willing to forsake our old ways.

*

Only prostrate, on the knees of our soul, might we receive revelation.

In insecure times, mystics are branded heretics and heretics pronounced holy.

*

It's the difficult fate of unwitting heretics to gloriously blaspheme in the name of the Most High.

*

Far better an impostor in the eyes of men and a true mystic in the eyes of G–d than vice versa.

*

Mysticism and occultism might appear similar; the chief difference is that the latter does not ask whence vision is granted.

The higher the leap, the greater the pitfall. Mysticism mispracticed can be akin to evil.

*

Every Messiah is reluctant—at least initially.

*

The sight of blackened lungs is enough for some smokers to alter their lifestyle. If we could see the state of our soul, would we change our lives?

*

Properly perceived, persecution is a position of privilege.

The greatest incentive to cease our heedlessness
is to alleviate the suffering of G–d.

✳

Practice self-confidence as a courtesy to others, since
to indulge in its opposite might be an imposition.

✳

Remember, it is always those with low self-esteem
that try to diminish ours.

✳

It is an extension of selfishness not to forgive others
what we do not forgive ourselves.

Part of forgiving is, eventually, forgetting.

*

To forgive is radical and visionary—it not only overlooks the past but also sets aside the need for justice in the interest of a better future.

*

Why announce to the world your few good deeds when you hide your many bad ones (even from yourself)?

*

To elicit envy we must be guilty, to some degree, of immodesty.

Remember, where there is envy, there is admiration grown sick.

✻

Envy is a hurdle to be cleared; on the other side lays emulation.

✻

The prayers most likely to be answered are selfless ones that we make for others.

✻

Love or prayer that is self-conscious is like kissing with our eyes open.

Our most profound prayers hardly reach our lips;
they are made with our entire being.

✳

A sign of profundity? When the horizon of a soul
appears to recede as we approach it.

✳

Scars are treasure chests.

✳

If "the wound is the place where the Light enters us,"
then we must keep our wound clean.

In exposing our wounds, healing begins.

✳

Prayer is also anesthesia, so that we might cut deeper, and clean out our wounds.

✳

If your wound is through no fault of your own, try and honor it by living bravely.

✳

When in doubt, meditate upon your wound.

If we gaze deeply into our own wound, we also see
the wounds of others.

✳

Whether we know it or not, all our love poems are
addressed to the Divine.

✳

All true poets are Caedmon, and all true poems hymns.

✳

In life's exams, it's no use straining to copy the answers
of another, since we are assigned different questions.

Questions as quests.

✳

The educated are schooled in the ways of the heart;
the literate are versed in the alphabet of emotions.

✳

To separate style from sincerity is cynicism.

✳

Style: the tip of that iceberg, substance.

If our hearts should harden and turn to ice, we must try, at least, not to blame the weather.

*

Bitterness: an unconscious admission of defeat.

*

Spiritual wisdom is to take no credit, yet assume all blame.

*

Be wary of those reluctant to assume blame, yet eager to accept credit.

Aphorisms are headlines, yes, but they are also the entire stories.

✳

Love does not smother—it watches over us from a safe distance.

✳

As true love deepens, shyness recedes.

✳

Intimacy obliterates our inhibitions.

There is a frequency peculiar to extreme states,
spiritual or sensual, that only the similarly afflicted
can pick up on.

*

If you wish to be heard, speak kindly. The same holds
true in speaking to ourselves.

*

We steal from ourselves when we share an idea or
a feeling before it has ripened.

*

Heart like a minefield: one misstep and . . .

Sometimes, not to take a step backward can be like taking a step forward.

∗

Sunlight is the best disinfectant, because secrets fester.

∗

See the sun, how it shifts the light of its attention gradually from one thing to the next. Be like it—don't fixate.

∗

Truth-telling always comes at a personal cost. The greater the truth, the greater the cost.

Wisdom is overhearing ourselves.

✳

The more closely we listen to ourselves, the more
likely we are to overhear others.

✳

Think of existence as a great love story; every shy
creature or timid truth wants to be courted.

✳

Every secret wants to be told; cultivate the
art of listening.

If we listen, the air is heavy with poems, ripe for plucking.

✳

To evolve means we've been listening.

✳

Evolution is a metaphor. We all begin as apes in this lifetime—the unfortunate among us remain on all fours.

✳

How evolution is like a video game: If we play well, we are promoted to higher levels and afforded greater opportunities or rewards.

Signs of spiritual evolution? That our slighter transgressions torment us for longer.

✳

Evolution is becoming ever more subtle.

✳

Be, all ways, becoming.

✳

To avoid the panic of last minute, practice readiness.

If we ask life for favors, we must be prepared to return them.

✳

Miracles are allotted in proportion to our trust.

✳

Just as mysteriously as spiritual favors are granted, so they may also be revoked.

✳

Wings are, always, on loan.

Those whom life trusts, she tells a secret or two.
If they betray her, she is slow to trust again.

✳

What this age seems to need most? Motivation!
(How else to explain the prevalence of life coaches:
the good, bad and dubious?)

✳

Does the contemporary mushrooming of "life coaches"
mean life can no longer be relied upon to do her job?

✳

Love is the true life coach—the rest are assistants
or impostors.

In a spiritually hungry and impatient age, the student is mistaken for a teacher.

✻

Only in an age of marketing is it desirable for a human being to become a brand.

✻

A sign of our unfocused, impatient times is that essays are now called "long reads."

✻

"Are we there yet?" The mantra of childhood and spiritual immaturity.

Personality, like scaffolding, is useful up to a certain point. Past that, it is an impediment to our development.

✷

We scramble the first half of our lives to assemble a self. And in the second half, if we are wise, to dismantle it.

✷

Behind what's referred to as personality—buoying it up, and determining its worth—is the force of our being.

Provocation is a spice of communication; it should be applied sparingly.

✳

Those who speak ill of life do not realize that they only smear their own names.

✳

As with any wild animal, it's unwise to turn our back to life.

✳

We are animals that pontificate about what we do not understand.

Human: the animal that requires medication to eat, sleep, make love, dream, be.

✳

Some worry about dying with wealth unused—far worse to live with love unspent.

✳

The degree of one's fear or worry attests to the extent of their faith.

✳

The best way to spoil a marriage is to speak too often and easily of it; likewise, with faith. Love and work grow strong in secret soil.

Conspiracy theories: misshapen offspring of
the all-but-impotent.

*

Hand over your reins to the One you trust; there's
freedom in harness.

*

Rebellion is adolescent; acceptance is maturity.

*

To struggle is to get further ensnared: surrender.

Surrender: the only choice we need to make.

✳

The person who knows how to accept will taste a
hidden sweetness in suffering.

✳

Accept the setback or calamity, and it is lifted
or transformed.

✳

Not by pushing does one get ahead, but by allowing
oneself to be pulled by the constant tug of all things.

Branches are roots, too, in the sky.

✳

Maybe we are upside-down trees, and our branches
in this world are roots in the next.

✳

If not before, we discover our roots when they
are being yanked at.

✳

There is no formula for truth-seeking—each time,
we must sharpen our tools and try a new one.

One might tell their truth through a fluidity of masks, but persona is a mask that has hardened in place.

*

There is body-time, and spirit-timelessness. We have all the time in the world.

*

Life is a time-release capsule, granting us only glimpses of ourselves at a time.

*

Our lives are like a long day; it's easier to fall sleep if we've remained awake.

Insomnia: the curse of those who sleepwalk
during the day.

*

Said a mystic to a hedonist: You would exchange
this celestial feast for your earthly crumbs?

*

Every day we're offered this world or the next, but
we cannot be myopic and farsighted at once.

*

We cannot faithfully love two—it's either this world
or the next.

Whether or not we're aware of it, our biography is perpetually being written—by the books on our shelves.

*

Signs of book addiction: a sense of homelessness after completing a book, or mounting malaise—until taking refuge in the next book covers.

*

The world is a book and those who do not read works by other cultures remain on the same page.

*

Pace yourself in relation to the race—if you're aiming for eternity, don't rush.

How the hours modulate their voice: from dawn's tremulous hope to dusk's winsome ache . . .

*

The challenge is to honor our sacred, half-dreaming intimations in forgetful or irreverent hours.

*

Every mood carries its power and insight, which is why we must try to work through them all.

*

Try to carefully guard your thoughts: they might be secreted to others in our dreams and beyond.

For those who discount dreams, consider this:
Relationships might be initiated, or altered,
while we sleep.

*

Dreams: the poor man's therapy sessions.

*

Dreams are evidence of wrestling with an invisible other.

*

The great whale hunt of the spirit life is also pursued
in dreams.

"Thou shalt not kill" begins with your spirit and extends to your dreams.

*

As we sleep, no one can steal from our dreams and sell them to another. So it is with our waking dreams; they are inviolable.

*

We are the guardians of our dreams.

*

Don't wake a sleepwalker, they say. The same applies to natural-born daydreamers: children, artists, thinkers, mystics, lovers, or revolutionaries.

Every newborn is a new opportunity to rewrite history.

*

After drunkenness, worldly or spiritual, comes a
higher sobriety.

*

A great artist is composed of three: the reckless drunk
who creates, the professional bore who edits, and the
heartless critic who assesses.

*

In the same way you can hear the sea in a conch shell,
if you press your ear against a work of art, you may
overhear the artist's spirit tossing and turning.

If you wish to know an artist better, try living with
their obsessions.

*

Utopia is to live in a world where the only terrorists
are artists.

*

Corrupt leadership creates terrorism and, through
terrorism, seeks to justify its continued existence.

*

True artists disturb the false peace, also known
as complacency.

Self-peace: our first step towards world peace.

*

The path to peace is littered with dead selves.

*

False divisions among mind/body/soul are the
origins of perversions.

*

Perhaps the work we are put here to do is to detach
ourselves from our finite bodies, so that we might
one day live, infinitely, as pure spirit.

It is a perversion of human nature that bullies, big and small, seek to play the role of victim.

*

Whether in world politics, or personal relations, the jailer is never free.

*

Revolutions are about overthrowing the tyranny of old fears—dictators are merely stubborn symbols of these.

*

There is no lasting revolution without spiritual evolution.

Beyond self-confidence, there is a deeper assuredness:
life-confidence. Past that, still another, unshakable trust.

*

Fear of success betrays a greater self-mistrust than
fear of failure.

*

The way to tame what is wild in us is to nurture
it fearlessly.

*

It's easier to be fearless when we remember that
we are deathless.

Everything beautiful is needful of our protection.

✳

When we behave unbeautifully, we give others
permission to do so, too.

✳

We write what we do not know but need to learn.

✳

Chasing silence is like embarking on a whale hunt. If one
actually catches up with this creature of the depths,
there's the danger of being swallowed whole.

Perhaps it is not poetry that purifies the language of the tribe, but silence.

✳

Words need not be the opposite of silence; they can be its ambassadors.

✳

Would that we could rescue the profundity of silence for our speech.

✳

We suffer from mass logorrhea. Memoirs and blogs are twin afflictions of our literary times.

To maintain immaculate speech, oftentimes silence is required.

✳

He was such a good listener; silence was too loud for him, for the din within.

✳

A cluttered mind makes for a poor mirror.

✳

Mind: the handrail we clutch in the dark for fear of falling. Yet it's precisely what trips us up where the stairs diverge.

Our rational mind would sooner accept a believable lie than an incredible truth.

*

The mind, needing to do its gymnastics, makes monkey bars of all things.

*

The heart is patient with the mind, because it knows better.

*

Our burden is made lighter if, instead of privileging it with "Why me?", we add it to the common load.

Best stress remedy? Trust that we are in good hands.

＊

Anxiety is a lack of trust, worry a lack of faith.

＊

Maybe it's not the future that fortune tellers read,
but our own longing concealed from us.

＊

Trust in longing to sing itself.

Longing: appetite not meant to be sated.

*

Like physical hunger, our spiritual appetite renews itself regularly.

*

One definition of success might be: refining our appetites while deepening our hunger.

*

To remain spiritually fit, practice Remembrance.

For our corporeal organs, there are corresponding
subtler, spiritual organs of perception.

*

The *Übermensch* is not Superman; he is the invisible man.

*

"Die before you die," a great teacher once said.
Philosophy, spirituality, parenthood, and aging all
offer us a chance to practice such dying to the self.

*

There's nothing unique about individuality.
Everyone's an individual.

The ultimate act of trust, in self and life, must be to have children.

∗

Live recklessly: trust.

∗

In life, as in relationships, if we trust, we are patient.

∗

Deliverance belongs to whoever can hold their breath the longest.

Hope is more patient than despair, and so outlasts it.

✳

Hope counsels: Every night, consent to die, again;
every morning, agree to be reborn.

✳

To anticipate the worst is to contribute towards
its realization.

✳

Pessimism poisons life's well, and then wonders
why it chokes.

Perhaps unbelievers are the burden of believers—
the way the underprivileged are the responsibility
of the privileged.

*

Pity atheists their pitilessness. They are like persons
hurt in love, who vow: Never again!

*

If the first casualty of war is truth, then a close second
is pity.

*

Wars are only possible when people are united by what
they hate, rather than what they love.

To love is to mirror shimmering possibilities—our own and those of the beloved.

✳

Even in parting, love bestows gifts: the transformative fires of separation.

✳

If love were not always a step ahead, how would it ensure we kept up the chase?

✳

We may not be faithful to lesser loves, but we cannot cheat on the One.

True love is the One we keep returning to.

*

We are ashamed only of false love; true love we declare from the rooftops.

*

When we think we've been thrown out of the nest, perhaps we've landed in a larger nest—whose perimeters are still too vast for us to perceive . . .

*

Can one be a mystic without religion? An update to the question posed by Camus: Can one be a saint without God?

There's mysticism in some poetry, yet there's poetry
in all mysticism.

✳

When the whole life of a poet is a poem, the poet
becomes a mystic.

✳

The dilemma of a mystical artist: How to create poetry
without words; how to sing soundlessly?

✳

We read the mystics not to escape religion,
but to illumine the holy books.

Dogma: a toll we pay on the way to freedom.

*

It is guilt that permits literalist interpretations of faith.
Those who believe we should go to hell have raised it
themselves on Earth.

*

To preoccupy ourselves with the shortcomings of the
religious is to lose sight of the marvels of religions.

*

The religious disposition: not to take credit for
anything, but to assume all blame.

If religions are properly understood as organized love, then, by definition, hate is heresy.

✳

An angry prayer is a contradiction in terms.

✳

A flying carpet is a prayer carpet.

✳

You, shaking your fist or wagging your finger, firstly, seek to become a luminous example—lastly, you may speak of religion and G–d.

Before you blaspheme, declaring yourself an agent of light acting in His Name, make sure you stand clear of your own shadow.

*

Atheism, as a season of the spirit, is equivalent to winter. Naturally, it should be followed by spring—where wonder stirs anew.

*

Eros: what makes eyes glisten or lines of verse shine.

*

How to acquire a third eye? Don't blink!

A lesson from the lives of saints: With Divine aid,
we are free to achieve the impossible. Without it,
we are prisoners of the laws of science.

✳

In the quotidian event, seek the theophany.

✳

All things—books, people, circumstances—might
be employed as mouths or arms to speak to us and
draw us closer to the Divine.

✳

Mysticism is a courtship.

There are books, like experiences, that measure our
distances and cannot be read until we reach their shores.

*

Those who only trust in their senses cannot differentiate
between magic tricks and true mystery.

*

So long as you trust in anything else, the miracle shall
be withheld.

*

Miracles are everyday occurrences, recognizing them
is not.

Logical interpretations are the miracle's modesty.

*

The guardian of the riddle must speak in riddles.

*

What is a mystic, but one who swoons, helpless in the face of beauty.

*

Sufism: the Romantic movement in religion.

Mysticism is beholding with Divine eyes.

✳

The mysticism of love unlocks secrets.

✳

Everything contains the secret to everything else.

✳

A loving gaze is sun, water, and soil for a soul to grow in.

We must try not to watch our hand when we give, create, love.

✻

To receive what we need most, we must first give it away.

✻

Even though we may switch stations or turn down the volume, love has no off button.

✻

The love we hold back in turn holds us back.

We only ever love once, though there are a hundred versions of it.

✳

Just be yourself, they say. Which one, I think?

✳

I do not think, therefore I am.

✳

Poetry is a way of speaking with others in hopes of overhearing ourselves.

It's not easy to speak to ourselves—we must devise ruses, interventions.

*

What we look for in a good book, painting, music, or conversation? A stretch of runway to take off and return us to ourselves.

*

Poetry is how we speak with ourselves.

*

It is not words, song, or art that are tremendous, but the human soul, and what is set in motion when it is stirred to the depths.

How to make pain hummable: the challenge of
popular music.

*

Bare necessity: a sturdy perch from which to watch
the world.

*

There is music that fills us with nostalgia for a past that,
otherwise, we would not recall.

*

The advice given Orpheus—never to look back until he
had reached the upper world—should be good enough
for us.

The self is a labyrinth at the heart of which awaits the spirit, hoping to be found.

✳

If you cannot shrink a subject, self-size in order to understand it; alternately, try to expand your understanding of self to encompass it.

✳

Entering into a debate with some is like stepping onto a moist wad of gum.

✳

Conversation, there's nothing like it—except silence.

Good conversations come from good silences, and
return there.

*

Remain silent, so that you might have something to say.

*

The privilege—and infinite challenge—of being one
of silence's spokespersons.

*

Talk is cheap, because it is the language of the body;
silence golden, since it's the native tongue of the spirit.

Poetry: the native tongue of hysterics—adolescents and mystics alike.

✳

Unlike prose, poetry can keep its secrets.

✳

Aphorisms are the marriage of heaven and hell: poetry and philosophy.

✳

Aphorisms are the parents of essays, and the children of poems.

Essays are like beached whales; poetry is the living ocean.

✳

We are captive to what we create.

✳

Art alters the artist and, in time, recreates them in its own image.

✳

Artists must believe—dependent as they are upon the mysticism of inspiration.

Artists are like mystics; they lower their buckets deep
into our communal well to retrieve what we thirst for.

✳

To become a mystic is not impossible; one must only
endure being a beggar, mad and dead.

✳

Spirituality: the art of harnessing almost
unbearable sensations.

✳

Mysticism: the disappearing act that takes a lifetime.

It is possible to subsist entirely on a diet of honey and wine, aka poetry and mysticism.

*

Know your muse, and its diet.

*

Think of the muse as beyond good and evil.

*

Our character shapes all our relationships—including that with the muse.

The true poet and mystic are not too proud to admit that in matters great and small they cannot proceed until they receive further instructions.

✳

When the voices are silent, confess ignorance.

✳

Writers write to silence the voices in their head.

✳

Finding your voice, as an artist, means choosing one.

The difference between a thinker and a mystic? A thinker mistakes epiphanies for their own.

*

We must be careful not to mistake our self for ourself.

*

Materialism and individualism: two synonyms for "dead-end."

*

Mysticism teaches us that if we can hold our breath long enough, we may breathe underwater.

Like all inspiration, mysticism relies on direct
transmission—one knows without knowing how.

✳

There's no substitute for inspiration. All that is required
is to be worthy to receive the muse.

✳

Those periods we refer to as dry spells are often secretly
fertile—when our very souls are being rewritten and
readied for fresh utterance.

✳

The monasticism of art: tension between inspiration
and self-denial.

Art is the love we make by ourselves, says the ego.
Art is the love we make with an invisible other,
replies the spirit.

✳

Morning dew: testament to the Eternal Gardener's
invisible care.

✳

In marriage, it is always the guilty party that praises
more extravagantly.

✳

Extravagant speech sounds extra vacant.

Big egos are easily played by little fingers.

*

Flatterers like to be flattered—flattery is their way
of letting you know it.

*

Rich praise, like rich food, is difficult to digest.

*

Boasting: what we do as our powers are waning.

Vanity never blushes.

✻

Funny how vanity, in fretting over appearances, renders us the butt of the joke.

✻

Narcissism requires keeping a distance from one's reflection—an inch closer, and the love spell is broken.

✻

Notice how what is highest and lowest in you, spirit and ego, borrow your mouth to speak—sometimes, at the same time.

There goes the ego again, pretending it is star-gazing when it is navel-gazing.

✳

Ego: a proud and choosy beggar.

✳

Celebrating birthdays is an unconscious acknowledgment of the mystery of astrology.

✳

Art needs no introductions; it makes its own friends.

We have art as a consolation for not having wings.

*

Spirituality knows which secrets are worth keeping.

*

Mystic: a shepherd of secrets.

*

Past the easy charm, the power charisma exerts over us is the intimation that another guards a secret—oftentimes, an inner life.

Our inner work is not the secret we suspect it to be—its essence is communicated energetically.

✳

There is a way to sanctify each moment: attention.

✳

To live attentively is to carry the sum of all we know in our minds and hearts at all times.

✳

Attention: a tension.

To grab attention and to hold it are two different things.

*

The anxious sense of missing out on something more important than what we are doing is a sign that we do not fully inhabit the present moment.

*

By being present to even humble tasks we are, paradoxically, transported.

*

Conversion from material to spiritual beings is ongoing—lifelong.

The pilgrim soul precedes the sacred site.

✳

Certain spaces retain a near presence of the Divine—like warm seats, recently vacated.

✳

There is a species of literature—poetry, especially—that aspires towards a form of sacred text.

✳

Literature is not a life sentence; writers may make a jailbreak or, based on good behavior, be released early.

With innocent grandiosity, poetry wonders: Can
we reorder the world by rearranging the words in
a sentence?

✳

The highest function of literature is transformational.

✳

Poetry is never a personal enterprise; a poet sings for
those who cannot.

✳

There is poetry, and then there is poetry.

Poetry, versus prose, is always an architectural marvel—how it speaks in between the lines.

✳

Part of the definition of an aphorist is one who spots aphorisms, and releases them from prose—the way Michelangelo described his sculpting process as freeing the angel from the marble.

✳

If there is any honor in being a poet, it's that of endurance. Enduring the devastation of poetry when it withholds and, more so, when it delivers.

✳

One never becomes a poet, except when they are writing a poem.

The demon honors you by their attentions; seek to become a worthy foe.

✷

Where there are demons, there is something precious worth fighting for.

✷

We can still become who we once were.

✷

To aestheticize is to anesthetize.

Aphorisms are the echoes of our silences.

✳

Aphorisms are also metaphysical expense reports.

✳

To write is to bow is to pray.

✳

Bow so low and you kiss the sky.

What's better than one open, outstretched palm? Two.

✳

The heart is like a sky: clear one blessed moment,
then so many shifting clouds and sudden showers
followed by sunshine.

✳

Good art is enigmatic; it invites you to BYOE (bring your
own examples).

✳

Artistic ideal: to expose oneself in public, yet
remain inscrutable.

A true artist rarely grasps the full extent of
what they mean.

✳

Concern with the creative process attests to the
mystery at the heart of it.

✳

The higher the aspirations of a writer, the less of
an authority they are on their work.

✳

Artists are parasites, their independence a myth
tolerated by countless hosts.

Please forgive neat-freaks; they are artists manqué,
after a kind of perfection.

✳

Freedom is not needing to have an opinion on everything.

✳

Our ego does not return the care we lavish upon it;
eventually, it will betray us.

✳

It's good for the ego to receive repeated blows,
until it bows.

If it can be inflated, it can be deflated.

*

In the cooking, ego and art are indistinguishable.
It's only afterwards that we're able to separate
the fat from the protein.

*

Ego: the baby rattle that becomes a snake rattle
if challenged.

*

Attachment: mistaking ourselves for our ego.

Ego, fed prime cut meats and rich sweets, leaves the rest of us with indigestion.

✳

Imagination devours everything, but the spirit is a fussy eater.

✳

The difference between drawing attention to one's self and a cause? A hairline.

✳

Writing: talking to the page like it's the last person on Earth.

Writing is live performance, scripted.

✳

To write is to shed skins—spiritual striptease before a fully clothed audience.

✳

Writing is only partially realized until it's read and, fully so, once lived by.

✳

Poetry is what we say to ourselves when there's nowhere to hide.

Self-taught insofar that what I know, I learned
by writing.

✳

There are many ways to donate blood; writing is one.

✳

Certain strains of writing serve as a form of life
support, stretched across space and time to sustain
world-weary readers.

✳

The ardent reader goes to confession every time
they pick up a pen and, helplessly, bares their soul
in the book margins.

The deeper we delve into our inner journey, the less
we are heard by the uninitiated.

*

The ideal reader is one who keeps pace with the
author, and does the inner work necessary to appreciate
the outer work.

*

A good reader is also a clairvoyant, communing
with spirits.

*

My ideal reader? One who does not read books.

How the great dead could articulate our nascent longing
before us—the minor miracle of books.

✳

Ideas dress themselves; writers are just the
helpless tailors.

✳

The play of ideas is eternal. We merely shuffle onstage
and off to introduce them to one another.

✳

Should distress persist, it's not enough to hold our
breath. We must learn to breathe underwater.

There is a special wisdom that is an offshoot of suffering,
like genius that is salvaged from the jaws of madness.

*

There are, of course, many degrees in madness.
Philosophy, psychology, and literature, to name but a few.

*

Mysticism: a controlled madness.

*

The difference between philosophy and spirituality?
For the latter, theory means little without practice.

Even the numinous, if not handled with caution,
can be ruinous.

✳

Superstitions: other people's traditions.

✳

If one's first love is for letters, people tend to
come second.

✳

Certain cherished books are like old loves. We didn't
part on bad terms, but it's complicated and would
require too much effort to resume relations.

One can be addicted to reading, and suffer withdrawal symptoms—irritability or emptiness—until that first delicious hit of words.

✳

We can never dip into the same book twice—it is always changing, along with us.

✳

Good reading is an active sport, like playing tennis with the author; we must try to send our all soaring over the net.

✳

Sports, and arts, cultivate and refine our appetites, teaching us how to admire the human form.

Art teaches us to admire without desire—so that, in turn, we might gaze at the world with such refined detachment.

*

The lover is strongest who desires least.

*

The extent of our pride determines our capacity to give and receive love.

*

Tranquility begins on the other side of commitment.

Paths are also relationships—to be meaningful,
they require fidelity.

✳

Spiritual tourists: the playboys of religions.

✳

It's all very well being a spiritual tourist—keeping in
mind that you cannot know a place until you
live there.

✳

If we pay attention, we are ushered along our path
in winks and nudges.

Every day we cast the net, and only what is ours returns to us.

✳

To enter every day with empty hands, trusting you will receive what you need—such is spiritual poverty.

✳

There is such a thing as spiritual deformity, a kink in the soul that keeps us from loving straight.

✳

Selfish love fosters dependence—hobbling the beloved, and then offering a crutch.

Cruelty: obscene pain turned outwards.

✳

The worst insult in the arsenal of cynics is: "You're naïve."
Nothing is more unfathomable, and threatening, to the
cynical than stubborn hope.

✳

To accept the world as it is isn't realistic, it's cynical.

✳

Since they make no allowances for happy surprises,
cynics are forever being surprised.

The danger of cynicism is getting what you believe in: nothing.

✳

Destiny, like our reflection in the mirror, will not permit being stared at overlong.

✳

In the same way that people are sensitive to condescension, fate is repelled by cynicism.

✳

Cynicism's knowingness cheats itself out of true knowing.

How tiresome to pass through life with one eyebrow perpetually arched.

✳

Cynicism: a knowingness that does not realize it lacks spiritual stamina; a shortage of breath and vision.

✳

Cynics are in need of constant reassurance. First, that their worst doubts about humanity are true and then, of course, that they are not.

✳

Cynicism is always cracking jokes—out of sheer terror.

Cynicism loves misery's company.

※

Cynics never win, because they insist on defeat.

※

In the spiritual dimension, versus the merely literary, one cannot produce a masterpiece without becoming one.

※

At a certain altitude, if our wings are large and powerful, there is no need to flap them—we simply soar.

To remain in fine flying form, our wings require careful, constant grooming.

✳

Wings are needed not only to fly, but also to keep our balance.

✳

No grace is possible—physical or spiritual—without attention.

✳

As in the physical realm, so in the spiritual—it takes one moment of inattention to slip and fall.

Early detection of spiritual tumors can lessen suffering and also save lives.

*

Spiritual initiation is knowledge received intravenously.

*

Gnosis teaches: it is only by knowing that we know.

*

Paradox: where truths hide in plain view.

On one level, the path to peace is self-remembering; on another, it is self-forgetting.

✳

As social animals, we need one another to reflect upon our interconnectedness and existential solitude.

✳

The paradox of enlightenment: To see our reflection in everything, and not to see our reflection in everything.

✳

The paradox of free will—we exercise it when we surrender to Divine will.

Mistrust your lower self and do not act as its bribed defender. It does not have your best interests in mind.

*

There are two ways through: one is fiendish complexity, the other is utter simplicity.

*

Strange, the power of the past—how our spiritual ancestors become, in turn, our influences.

*

Wisdom is the obliteration of false distinctions, like opposites.

Contradiction: the preferred cloak of profound truths.

*

I've only ever been interested in contradictions—which
is to say, everything.

*

Unattended, things may become their opposites—the
way rebellion can curdle, and turn (back) into conformity
or enslavement.

*

Atheism, which may start as a step towards establishing
our independence, can become a form of slavery
if it lingers.

Punishment for those who stand on life's sidelines
sneering shall be that they stood on life's
sidelines sneering.

✷

Walking meditation—try to leave everything in your
path in slightly better shape than you found it: the
home in disarray, the neglected pet, the lonely neighbor,
the homeless person on the bench, the hungry birds
in the parking lot, the despondent stranger in the
elevator, the overworked elder at the checkout, the
trash-littered sidewalk, the overturned shopping carts . . .

✷

Fear of ridicule keeps us mediocre.

✷

Mediocrity does not recognize itself, especially if it's
also ambitious.

136

If you are original or profound, there is no need to bemoan the mediocrity of the times we live in—your work will stand out in relief.

✳

In short-sighted times, we can only hope that history will have better foresight than us.

✳

One can trick their own time, but they cannot fool history.

✳

We do not choose our work, we merely consent to it.

By remembering the light, we might smile in the dark.

✳

If we smile at frightening things, they may go away—but if we dare to laugh, they might join us.

✳

Laughter wears its courage lightly.

✳

God is the ultimate realization that there is nowhere left to hide and no one else to turn to.

In our inverted era, the love that dare not speak its name
is Divine.

*

The grades of love we are ashamed to confess: from the
playground crush to Divine madness.

*

Jealousy is Divine.

*

A word to would-be writers (including those widely
published): Attitude alone is not style.

Style is art we quietly make out of our entire being; attitude merely a form of loud withholding.

*

Attitude: the clanky armor of the emotionally handicapped.

*

There is such a thing as spiritual clutter and hoarding, too.

*

Infatuation, as any hothouse flower, will only flourish in a climate-controlled environment. A degree more or less and it withers.

We make daily negotiations with others just to keep alive—whether having sex, or crossing the street.

*

In the darkest night, there blooms a luminous white rose.

*

Hope: the window we turn to when the living room turns on us.

*

Hope never tires of reminding us that what seemed impossible yesterday is, again, likely today.

Seeds: the little that life needs to create hope.

*

Excuses: the first refuge of a failure.

*

We must try not to take our fight with ourselves out into the world.

*

Activist: an angry person in search of a cause.

Knowing ourselves is a basic courtesy to others, especially those we love.

*

The better we know ourselves—who we are and what we want—the less likely we are to hurt others.

*

When we think we are arguing with others, we are usually arguing with ourselves.

*

There's nothing virtual about connection.

Virtual world: real emotions in real time.

*

There are virtual vultures as well, who appear online only when they suspect someone is down.

*

In our media circus, it's often the clowns that are taken seriously.

*

Never meet your heroes, the saying goes. The same can be true on social media.

Social media: a chance for the masses to practice the writer's ruse—creating an aspirational persona.

✳

Facebook: where we go to deceive others, and end up believing our own illusions.

✳

Addressing an imaginary audience used to be considered madness. Now it's called social media.

✳

The poignancy of persons speaking to themselves in public—how the virtual world mirrors the real.

Smartphones: modern worry beads.

＊

One of the curiosities of social media is how, increasingly, we turn to virtual strangers to fulfill our intimate needs.

＊

In an age of voyeurism, social media is how we keep our diaries.

＊

Licensed eavesdropping is what social media offers us, as partners in humanity.

If we rise to the challenge, social media affords us the opportunity to be researchers of the human condition, as well as citizen journalists.

✳

The seduction of social media—a taste of omniscience.

✳

Social media: the art of living out loud.

✳

Social media might make us feel less lonely, but it also makes it more difficult to be alone.

Social media: our fear of being silent and alone.

✳

Character is what we are in company; alone, we
are everyone.

✳

Past exhibitionism, social media stands to teach us a
subtle truth: At heart, there is no distinction between
private and public communication.

✳

Nowadays, most of us lead double lives online.

Twitter: ballroom of dancing consciousnesses.

✳

A tweet as a sign of virtual life, signaling: "I'm here,
I still exist."

✳

Before Twitter, hardly anyone knew what an aphorism
was. After Twitter, almost everyone suspects they are
an aphorist.

✳

The pressures of modern life: Nowadays, it's not
enough to have fun, or be in love if it's not photogenic
or instagrammable.

Love in the digital age: I hang on your every tweet.

*

A watched tweet is never retweeted.

*

Emoticons: a crisis of faith in language.

*

Emoticons: technical assistance for the emotionally
hard of hearing.

Smiley faces: canned laughter for our digital age.

*

Online communication can be like two people trying
to hug while wearing bulky sweaters. You must do it
with intention to feel the warmth.

*

Netiquette: the virtual measure of an individual's
real social and emotional intelligence.

*

How we conduct ourselves online can be as
unconsciously revealing as body language.

Pets: proof positive that communication and love are not dependent on language.

*

We are not alone—countless creaturely friends await us in the wings.

*

In speaking to others, and ourselves, we are more likely to be heard if we whisper than if we bark.

*

Before roaring some great truth, practice whispering it.

A whisper is like a kiss.

*

Intuition asks: What use are two open eyes when you're in the dark?

*

History is like family—in times of crisis, you rush to its side before pausing to think.

*

Nations are like families, too, in that if we felt emotionally safe and had space to grow, we'd never have run away in the first place.

Those ignorant of history are doomed to repeat it—hence, the tragedy of families.

*

History teaches us, and world news reports confirm, that not all deaths are equal; there is an exchange rate for human lives as well.

*

Selective moral outrage is another name for hypocrisy.

*

While the number of celebrities mounts, that of saints remains constant throughout the ages.

The lazy lust for celebrity gossip is a form of shirking the hard work of self-knowledge.

✳

Gossip is a drug, and those who listen are enablers.

✳

Gossip: spiritual cannibalism.

✳

Shoot the messenger if they are a relayer of gossip.

Perhaps what lies behind attraction, even erotic,
is a disguised lust for self-knowledge.

*

How to attract a kindred spirit? Secrete your secret,
and they will recognize the scent.

*

Spiritually, too, we secrete pheromones that
attract others.

*

There exists a spiritual equivalent in humans to the
"egg tooth" in young birds, which also develops at
the needed time to assist us in breaking free from
our shell, and escaping into new life.

Birds are a reminder to stretch our wings.

*

Self-criticism is easy on a superficial level, indulgent even. The deeper sort is harder; that wounds our pride and tenderly incubated self-image.

*

Eloquence is morally neutral.

*

What a tragedy to share one's wisdom with everyone—except oneself.

Knowledge is amoral; it can lead to wisdom or lead
one astray. Yet wisdom entails moral knowledge.

✳

Wisdom is becoming innocent once more.

✳

To truly begin again requires utter humility.

✳

To innocence, all things are permitted.

Arrogance is an untenable position; life brings us all to our knees.

✳

For every "I don't," try to atone with an "I do" or two. With "I do" is how we marry the world.

✳

In matters big and small, the arrogance of "Why?" prevents an answer.

✳

It's not what you know, but what you are.

Our wants tend to scare things off—the more desperately we want a thing, the less likely we are to get it.

∗

Wanting: what mars the purity of a relationship, human or Divine.

∗

Papercuts: battle scars of the office clerk.

∗

Battlefield: where angels fear to tread.

The health of a society may be measured by the depravity
of its sickest members, and their numbers.

✳

If the healthy mind in a healthy body was the Greek
ideal, the inverse is the Modernist reality.

✳

Burdened by an unendurable present, and faced with an
unforeseeable future, the Modernist mind wanders to the
incomprehensible bliss of an idyllic past: innocence lost.

✳

How the present and future are always shuffling the
cards called "past" . . .

Gazing into the future is like staring at the sun—look
too long and it might blind you to the present.

*

When an emissary of the past addresses you—say,
an old love or friend—speak to them with the respect
and tenderness befitting a ghostly self.

*

Memory has its own geographies, not all of which can
be found on a map.

*

Within each of us resides an incorrigible fabulist
called memory.

We can easily become prisoners of certain memories.
Remember, there's freedom in forgetting.

✳

The right to free speech ends where hate speech begins.

✳

When hate speech is tolerated, eventually some
murderous fool acts out on the violence in the air
and latent in people's hearts.

✳

It's not the obscenity of swear words that's
objectionable, but their violence.

A bigot is a bigot—however much they may smell
like a rose.

✳

The bigot's crime is twofold: not knowing others well
enough to love them, and not knowing themselves
enough to recognize their own hatred.

✳

Outspoken bigots embolden quiet ones.

✳

Hate, too, is a species of love. Perhaps our enemies are,
after all, merely thwarted lovers.

Distortion in the work of Absurdists, Surrealists and other contortionists suggests a world view where the truly outlandish is that which passes every day for normal.

✳

Distortion in art is the artist's representation of the lack of proportion in life.

✳

It's not enough to love an art. For it to count as a relationship, the art must love you back.

✳

Art is a triumph over suffering—it is the longest-lasting painkiller.

Impulses, as with inspiration, cannot be summoned at will. Depending on our hospitality, they may feel more, or less, welcome to return.

*

Uninvited guests, like refugees, test the limits of our hospitality.

*

The inspiration for all our art? Mortality.

*

We are all victims of our temperaments, yet we are not treated equally on account of it.

Substance-induced drunkenness is milder than that other drunkenness . . . of the senses.

✳

Lust is the love that consumes itself.

✳

Desire never dies, which is why mystics shrewdly entrust it to the eternal.

✳

Desire is to the body what longing is to the spirit.

The body may deceive, but it does not lie.

*

Body: the great equalizer.

*

Could it be that philosophers so little address humor
and desire because they intuit the mind's helplessness
before a joke or wink?

*

Caricatures can be more revealing than portraits.

There are many ways to touch the depths;
lightheartedness is one of the most profound.

*

Between comedy and tragedy, a hairline the depth
of an abyss.

*

Burning love that is readily transferable from one
person to another is not love; it is desire.

*

Lust: torments of insatiability.

Fear is the father of greed. Promiscuity is born of
the incestuous union between greed and fear.

*

Obscenity: ambition without talent.

*

The only excuse for blind ambition is blinding talent.

*

Strange how our weaknesses can be strengths
in disguise, and vice versa.

You cannot refuel at the devil, and expect it to take you to G–d.

✳

What causes the devil's smugness? Our bad habits and addictions.

✳

Perhaps the devil is a metaphor for all those who refuse to bow.

✳

Do not be deceived, (d)evil has no loyalties.

Real difficulties are manageable; it's imaginary ones
that are insurmountable.

*

Illusion test: If you can hold it in your hand, then it's
not real.

*

The hell of the self subsides once we recognize
it's imaginary.

*

Hell is being trapped in the vicious cycle of our vices.

Before we can accumulate more energy, we must
stop up the holes where it escapes.

*

What do self-absorption, self-pity and
self-righteousness have in common? Self.

*

The antidote to self-indulgence is a sense of humor.

*

At the heart of every vice sits selfishness, yawning.

The best way to be rid of a temptation is not to entertain it as an option.

*

To yield, regularly, to temptation makes it difficult to regain mastery over oneself.

*

The human figure is sublime; perversity disfigures it.

*

To mate with the sublime, sublimate.

Abstinence is the aphrodisiac of the soul.

*

Complete honesty is the luxury of the utterly good,
or the utterly shameless.

*

Contrary to what popular culture would have us believe,
confidence and shamelessness are not synonymous.

*

In popular culture's commitment to amusing itself
to death, you can catch a whiff of sheer terror.

Fandom: popular culture's corruption of the religious impulse.

*

The stakes are higher for seekers—their capacity for virtuousness and baseness are intensified.

*

Our morality is determined by the level of immorality that we can afford to live with.

*

Good manners are the tip of the iceberg called morals.

Earplugs and eye masks are useless sleep aids when noise and chaos are on the inside.

✱

Conscience: the skewer and the spitfire.

✱

Conscience admonishes: The time you should spend sharpening your sword, don't waste polishing its sheath.

✱

Every time we betray our conscience, we strangle an angel. Yet it's not certain we are allotted an infinite supply of winged pardons.

Shield the angel, as you would a child, from seeing what is unbecoming.

✷

It's a sign of spiritual maturity when lesser transgressions prick our conscience more than before.

✷

Unheeded pricks of conscience might return as harpoons of circumstance.

✷

Inhibitions might be the handmaidens of conscience.

To breathe easier, do what is harder.

*

As with all battles, how we fight determines
who we become.

*

To win a battle, morally, seek to be as blameless
as humanly possible.

*

The deceiver promises short-term release while
tightening our shackles.

Enemies of the holy hush crouch nearby, ready to pounce. The quiet majesty of our wholeness disturbs them more than anything else.

✳

The devil's siren song has always been the same: "Let it all burn."

✳

Think of the devil as scared and all his counsel issuing from a place of desperation.

✳

Everything detects the scent of fear—even the nostrils of our future.

How vast the future that it can serve as bottomless
repository of all our fears, hopes and dreams . . .

✳

To keep our eyes, mind and emotions on a leash—this,
too, is freedom.

✳

"Don't even think it!"—a recognition of the power
of (negative) thinking.

✳

Questioning everything is good practice for, eventually,
accepting everything.

Acceptance is trying not to steal from each day, but to receive only what is freely offered.

*

Once we assent to life, ribbon and wrapping paper come undone.

*

Before asking for more, pause to recognize the prayers that have already come to pass.

*

Gratitude is caring for what we've been granted.

How attentive the forces of darkness; how they rush
to answer our ill-conceived wishes.

✳

Shrewdness dictates some sort of faith as a creative
force, versus the destructiveness of doubt.

✳

Doubts are shadows, grown bold in the absence of light.

✳

Strange, how one hate enables another—how they
are like unconscious allies, darkly united in blocking
out the light.

As you progress to the light, notice how jealous shadows also redouble their efforts.

*

In most cases, darkness is a choice; the light is worth fighting for, and hard.

*

When in doubt, meditate: on what's come to pass that you thought impossible, and what's not that you thought possible.

*

Discipline: how we tame our suffering.

To manage our suffering portfolio, it helps to know
what we can afford spiritually.

*

Suffering is inevitable; there is no need to contribute
to it—our own or others'.

*

Buoyancy of the human spirit in the face of turbulence
is the source of the miraculous.

*

There's some music in words, more music in sounds;
then there's that other, soundless music.

Words have a certain charge—the deeper they remain with us, the closer they are to life's core, and the more likely they are to reach strangers.

✳

In serving words faithfully, we also serve one another.

✳

Like incantations, certain word combinations can set a sentence or soul in motion.

✳

How time ravages us . . . and hardship, like genius, accelerates this process.

To grow older is to grow tired ... of pretending.

✳

Getting older is realizing that we've been repeating ourselves all along.

✳

Turning forty: when we begin to repeat ourselves and, hopefully, to overhear ourselves as well.

✳

Turning forty: when our free pass, aka unconscious living, is revoked.

Forty: the adulthood of youth and youth of old age.

*

Forty: when the fruit that is our body starts to spoil
and the rose tree of our soul begins to bloom.

*

Our forties: when our bodies begin to prepare us
for dying.

*

In the deep end, every stroke counts.

Those for whom the natural is extraordinary tend to find the extraordinary natural.

✳

Adolescence: the forbidden fruit that we must all taste and suffer the loss of our innocence.

✳

"Paradise," as a symbol, represents what we are denied in our earthly existence. To the seeker, this means homecoming.

✳

Philosopher as outsider: how else to evaluate the play—onstage, alongside other actors?

The artist must cultivate a certain distance so that they might lend their vision to others.

*

Artists are heralds, registering an advancing stranger called Change.

*

Our salvation lies on the other side of our gravest danger.

*

To sense we are always at a great turning point is a sign of spiritual vitality.

There is a point in unlearning, where we cannot proceed any further without transformation.

*

The price of transformation is nothing less than our old life.

*

At times we must look away if we are to have something to say.

*

Treat life as seriously as you would a dress rehearsal. No more, no less.

This is the symbolic life; the previous and the next are the real.

✳

What we love in the next world, we begin by loving here, first.

✳

If in this life no person can save another, how much more so that must apply to the next life . . .

✳

Perhaps the most we can achieve in this life is to trace the dim impressions of the last, so that we might be free to move on to the next.

Everything we do here matters elsewhere.

✳

To be—here and elsewhere—that is the challenge.

✳

Words, like us, must do their work here first—on their
way to somewhere else.

✳

Heaven save us from tragic seriousness. Teach us
to play divinely.

Perhaps crisis is self-induced disaster—a last-ditch effort we gift ourselves to, finally, transform.

✳

Best not flirt with disaster, lest it decide to commit.

✳

Civilization is carefully stitched together, yet easily undone. Humans, too, are a form of organized chaos, capable of unraveling for an instant or a lifetime.

✳

We're here to pass around the ball of light, while keeping our fingerprints off it.

Modernism and Existentialism: a two-headed monster.

*

No matter how we dream or scheme, being born is always a surprise.

*

We cannot know ourselves without knowing the natural world.

*

Those who stop short and worship the natural world forget that nature, too, is following orders.

We run from You to You. There is nowhere else to go . . .

*

The instincts are a reminder of our animal nature;
the ability to resist them a reminder of our godly nature;
and the restless tension in-between is a reminder of
our human nature.

*

We may trust our instincts once we have tamed them.

*

The body betrays, but it does not lie.

Those who overhear us might serve as our conscience when we are in need of reminding.

*

We look to one another for cues on how to live with dignity and courage.

*

Share with others the lessons you are learning—chances are, they need them, too.

*

We are here to remind each other.

The only failures are misanthropes.

*

Our stubborn character defects ought to prohibit us from judging others.

*

A deceptively simple lesson, repeated throughout our days: learning when to say yes, and when to say no.

*

Meditation is knowing when to keep awake and when to fall asleep.

A lesson to bullies, big and small: Controlling others is a spiritual impossibility. Those who try must exist in a state of existential insecurity.

*

Power can corrupt; this we know. But beauty is a form of power, too, we mustn't forget.

*

There is something inherently tragic where beauty, power or greatness are concerned.

*

Mistrust a person without a sense of humor seeking power—it usually translates into a lack of mercy.

Politics: what makes smart people sound stupid
and stupid people sound smart.

*

Decadence: pleasure that derives from, and
returns to, pain.

*

It is a sign of cultural decadence when the fear of
being regarded a prude is greater than the shame
of appearing immoral.

*

Mercy is to cover the nakedness of others, and
stand beside them naked yourself.

Signs of mercy? How we continue to be spared, even rewarded, as we transgress.

✳

We are shamed into self-improvement when our transgressions are met with forgiveness and generosity. The stirrings of faith . . .

✳

The problem with being full of yourself is that you cannot fill up with much else.

✳

Vacate yourself, and you might become the site of a great event of the spirit.

Windicism: a statement that is more hot air than wit. Profound-sounding, but actually shallow.

✳

The wisest observation is also the humblest.

✳

To be free of the tyranny of time, one may try and take the lead.

✳

In close matches, the score is settled afterwards, in the overtime.

If variety is the spice of life, does that make monotony
the main dish?

*

Atheism, like any other religion, has its share of violent
extremists who misrepresent the peaceful majority and
give the faith a bad name.

*

Immaturity: atheism to the believer, and belief to
the atheist.

*

A believer is like a person in love—invincible, in a sense,
and helpless before the beloved.

Maturity is to care more for a precious few things, and less about much else.

*

Maturing is sweetening.

*

It is a sign of aging to overlook the real good in one's time in favor of an illusory past.

*

It's never quite the present that fails us, but our own powers.

One advantage of immaturity is youthfulness.

*

Growing older and growing up are not synonymous.

*

Growing up means complaining less.

*

One cannot complain and learn at the same time.

Middle age: when mortality is no longer an abstraction.

✳

There is freedom in not needing to possess what
you admire.

✳

Once we accept we do not own anything, we also realize
we cannot lose anything.

✳

Every day, in every way, we negotiate the parameters
of our freedom.

The best, and worst, type of person is one possessed
by a mission.

*

Stockholm syndrome begins at home.

*

To those who once held our peace of mind or self-worth
hostage, we may gently let them go with these words:
"I no longer accept your version of reality."

*

Perhaps peace is stillness over trembling.

What we refer to as "the real world" is often our failure of imagination.

∗

Reality is a rose of a thousand petals.

∗

Artist's compassion: imagining the lives of strangers.

∗

Compassion and contempt are not compatible.

You don't truly know someone's spirit until you've seen them dance—with abandon.

✳

Dancing is a form of exorcism.

✳

Airplane wisdom: "Make sure your oxygen mask is well adjusted, before helping others."

✳

"Please be careful when opening the overhead compartment, as items may have shifted during flight." Every time I hear this, the last thing I think of is luggage, but rather baggage, lost loves and past selves. Time, how it shakes us up, like a rattle . . .

Maybe, you can never go home again, but you can never leave home, either.

*

Sometimes, we need to take the opposite route to return home.

*

No matter how voluntary it may appear, exile is never really a choice.

*

Exiles always feel a little posthumous.

The art of exile, like dying or being reborn,
requires a life of practice.

*

The exile's love is absolute—it pines for an ideal.

*

An exile's love is never-ending, and we are all exiles.

*

Exile is the ink exiles dip into to write their poetry.

Artists are touched-up metaphors for everybody.

✳

Love has a myriad faces; impossible is one of them.

✳

Sensationalism simplifies by disguising emotion
as thought.

✳

Perspective: watching paint dry is the contrary
of boring—if you're a painter.

How opposites can appear similar: the military and
the monastery, both ways of surrendering our will,
becoming children and blindly following orders.

*

How militaries are a little like organized pedophilia:
corrupt elders seducing the young, abusing their minds
and bodies, then discarding them afterwards.

*

In wars, post-traumatic stress disorder can be
another name for conscience.

*

Pity that in the majority of alien movies, other life
forms visit to invade and destroy our planet. Perhaps,
when we can conceive of more peaceful, curious,
generous strangers, we will be less prone to invade
and destroy other countries.

Between amorality and immorality, a subtle step.

✳

However bad you think it is, it's not the end of the world.
We don't even know what the end of the world is.

✳

In the midst of chaos, recall what is indestructible.

✳

Parting paradox: We practice the art of living most fully
once we practice the art of dying.

Rigidity is the need to conclude. Let the last sentence of your soul stand open-ended . . .

The generous contributors below selected
a higher-level pledge to work on an aphorism
of their own with me. I hope you will enjoy
the results as much as I do.

Polish the shield of Loyalty often, lest it wear away under
the force of battle.

SAWSAN DAJANI

Persistence plucks all the strings of the heart until it
starts to sing.

SAWSAN DAJANI

Fear wants protection.
Anger wants destruction.
And love just wants to spread . . .

SHERINE GAMAL EL DINE

Don't miss the taste of wine on your lips—while dreaming
of imaginary vineyards.

JEHANE NOUJAIM

Time management is like a liquid; it takes the form of
its container.

ANNIE RESTREPO

Half of a solution is a good diagnosis.

PATTI RESTREPO

About the Author

YAHIA LABABIDI's 2016 book, *Balancing Acts: New & Selected Poems* (1993–2015), came in at number 1 on Amazon's Hot New Releases, and was featured on PBS *NewsHour*. Lababidi's first collection of aphorisms, *Signposts to Elsewhere* was selected as a 2008 Book of the Year by the *Independent* in the UK. Other books of his include a critically acclaimed collection of essays, *Trial by Ink: From Nietzsche to Belly-Dancing*; a series of ecstatic, literary dialogues with Alex Stein, *The Artist as Mystic: Conversations with Yahia Lababidi*; and a collection of short poems, *Barely There* (Wipf & Stock, 2013), inspired by the constraints of social media, and featured on NPR.

Lababidi's work has appeared in several anthologies, such as *Geary's Guide to the World's Great Aphorists*, where he is the only contemporary Arab poet featured; in the best-selling US college textbook, *Literature: An Introduction to Reading and Writing*; and, most recently, in *Short Flights*, the first anthology of modern American aphorists.

To date, his writing has been translated into several languages, including: Arabic, Hebrew, French, German, Spanish, Slovak, Italian, Swedish and Dutch. Lababidi has participated in international poetry festivals in the United States, Eastern Europe, and the Middle East, while video adaptations of his poems have been shown in film festivals worldwide.

Acknowledgments

Crowdfunding *Where Epics Fail* has been an exercise in humility and gratitude. Much appreciation to Unbound and all who kindly pledged, for teaching me how active readers can be in helping to realize the dream of an author. Beloved family, dear friends, and warm supporters, *this book is because you are.*

Selected aphorisms have appeared in the following publications/outlets:

PBS NewsHour, National Public Radio (NPR), *Best American Poetry*, *World Literature Today*, AGNI, *The Prague Revue*, *HuffPost*, *New Internationalist*, *Hotel Amerika*, *Journal of Baha'i Studies*, Idries Shah Foundation, *Elephant Journal*, Plough, *Kyoto Journal*, *Cutthroat*, *The Scofield*, *Portland*, *Mizna*, *PMC Magazine*, *Berfrois*, *Numero Cinq*, *Arts & Opinion*, *Writing Tomorrow*, *Trinacria*, *Crosstimbers* and *Caldera Culture Review*.

Praise for *Where Epics Fail*

The aphorisms in *Where Epics Fail* exhort us to pay attention, believe we can make a difference, keep our hearts open in the face of pain, take responsibility for our actions, avoid ego and do the hard work that comes with sticking to ideals.

ELIZABETH FLOCK, PBS *NewsHour*

Aphorisms are an ancient form, but its current-day master is Yahia Lababidi. Like a sip of wine, a wave just as it breaks, a sliver of the moon, or a drop of rain, each of Yahia's aphorisms appears as a simple, natural gesture, that in fact holds multitudes of meaning rooted in the eternal. See for yourself what I mean.

RICHARD BLANCO,
Barack Obama's historic inaugural poet

"Aphorisms respect the wisdom of silence by disturbing it, briefly." So writes aphorist Yahia Lababidi, reminding me that aphorisms and poems use the same means: poetry being the other literary form that speaks through its silences as much as through its words. In *Where Epics Fail*, Lababidi is an aphorist of the spirit. While his aphorisms have his personal stamp on them, they also transcend him to speak of timeless truths within the timely. They create microcosms that teach us how to inhabit them. His aphorisms could form a new gnostic religion, and I could dwell a long while inside them. Yahia Lababidi may be our greatest living aphorist.

SHARON DOLIN, author of *Manual for Living*

A clever aphorism can do a number of things. It can make you smile or frown; it can make you think or stun you into silence. A clever aphorism is immediately satisfying food, so that a diet of two or three each time one opens the book will usually suffice. An aphorism expresses a universal truth, but its poignancy comes from its personal particularity. The reader will see something about himself as well as about the universe around him. In that case, there will be as many people who are incapable of profiting from this collection of wise and witty aphorisms as there are people who are uninterested in themselves and the world about them. That is, none.

ROBIN WATERFIELD,
author of *Prophet: The Life and Times of Kahlil Gibran*

Yahia Lababidi punctures our little worlds of self, and when we peer through each pinprick we see a cosmos, a new one each time.

KEVIN HART, author of *Poetry and Revelation*

Egyptian-born Lababidi is a poet, aphorist, essayist and mystic. He is steeped in the traditions of Western philosophy but comes from a world where the desert reminds you constantly that you are surrounded by a vast inimical emptiness; the ancient Christian hermits used to sit in the Egyptian desert because from there you could place a toll-free call to Paradise ... Although it may seem contradictory to say so, the mystic is a person in conversation; everything in him burns toward that conversation.

DOUGLAS GLOVER, author of *Savage Love*

Lababidi['s] work is characterized by a contemplative tone in line with Rumi ... [He] is a Muslim voice for peace, celebrating the wisdom in ancient traditions and pointing out the ridiculous in the rush and cynicism of contemporary life. Drawn to the mystic tradition, Lababidi often refers to the virtues and fruits of silence.

Plough Quarterly

Lababidi's meditative formulations echo the inquiries of the early Greeks, Confucius, de La Rochefoucauld, Nietzsche, Pascal and Lao Tzu.

KEN RODGERS, *Kyoto Journal*

223

Praise for Previous Books

Yahia Lababidi writes as a man possessed with both the sayable and unsayable, as a poet "in search of that which is in search of him," as one of his mystical predecessors, Jalāl ad-Dīn Muhammad Rūmī, described the poet's unnegotiable mission. Like Walt Whitman, he believes in his soul and listens to it with prayerful attention, apprehending first "the hum of [his] valved voice" before conjuring his own original expression for the wedding dance of mystery and wisdom. His authority resonates in plain-spoken yet dazzling poetry—sometimes epigrammatic, sometimes expansive—that betrays the eclectic transmissions of his myriad influences, from Hafiz to Kierkegaard, Dickinson to Kafka. He is indeed a piece of wood that's found itself a violin, and yet he is not a violin that knows he's a violin. His poetry, music, and wisdom pass through him unselfconsciously, purely, like a hallowed breeze. He must hurt at the sound of his ecstasies.

CHARD DENIORD,
Poet Laureate of Vermont and author of *Interstate*

Lababidi moves from the aphoristic and the epigrammatic to the suggestive, the lightly hinted, the nuanced, with impressive ease. This is a rare gift, more associated with European writers than with American. This striation of tone, of register, of mood, gives a sense of surprise to his sentences; they spring back to the touch. Sometimes they even seem surprised at themselves ... The book becomes an exploration on which the reader embarks. This is one of the elements in collections I most appreciate—this secret invitation au voyage that the author holds out—and Lababidi does this extremely well, with courtesy as well as cunning.

ERIC ORMSBY, poet, scholar,
and author of *Ghazali: The Revival of Islam*

I find myself pausing everywhere among these wisdoms, wondering why the world stumbles and staggers through such a dark and greedy time when there are people alive with such keen, caring insight ... If Yahia Samir Lababidi were in charge of a country, I would want to live there.

NAOMI SHIHAB NYE, poet, anthologist,
and author of *There is No Long Distance Now*

Brilliant ... think of the wild mind of Blake and the calmly collected Wallace Stevens, with a touch of Franz Kafka's hammer inside a velvet glove.

DUFF BRENNA, novelist and
author of *Murdering the Mom: A Memoir*

226

Wisdom for Lababidi is on the move, a matter of supple-
ness rather than rigor, of insights and angles rather than
rules ... As intense as his conversation with himself is, it
is also kind, tolerant of his own limits and of ours ... I give
you that expert self-listener, that excellent writer, Yahia
Lababidi.

JAMES RICHARDSON, poet, aphorist,
and author of *By the Numbers*

Lababidi knows that fables and metaphors overcome
resistance more readily than facts and position papers.
His half-smile becomes our own, changing our self-
estimate, and then—who knows?—the choices we make
as well.

ALFRED CORN, poet, essayist,
and author of *Tables*

Supporters

Unbound is a new kind of publishing house. Our books are funded directly by readers. This was a very popular idea during the late eighteenth and early nineteenth centuries. Now we have revived it for the internet age. It allows authors to write the books they really want to write and readers to support the books they would most like to see published.

The names listed below are of readers who have pledged their support and made this book happen. If you'd like to join them, visit www.unbound.com.

Ouranitsa Abbas
Jehane Abdel Barry
Hoda Abdel-Hamid
Rhamy
   Abdel-Hamid
Mustafa
   Abdel-Wadood
Marie Therese
   Abdelmessih
Basma
   Abdelmoneim

Ehaab Abdou
Iman Abdulfattah
Larry Abel
Zain Abu
Drew Adams
Salma Adly
Vinita Agrawal
Sherif Ahmed
   Artisan
Michael Airhart
Claire Åkebrand

Maram Al-Jazireh
Lahab Assef
   Al-Jundi
Mai Al-Nakib
Tariq Al-Olaimy
Mirvat Alasnag
Badr Albanna
Mariam Ali
Sly Alley
Saif Alshamsi
Carrie Amestoy

Najla Amin
John Anania
M Khadija Anderson
Tayha Anderson Ms.
Jose Araguz
Alexandra Arah
Paul Archibald
Sanya Aroussy
Ayman Ashour
Carolyne Ashton
Leslie Asllani
Fatma Saleh Assef
David Ault
Kathryn Salaam
   Ayoob
Ayyud Ayyuda
Hani Badawi
Maura Badji
Fadia Badrawi
Donna Baier Stein
Gene Ball
Merate Barakat
Claire Barta
Russell Bennett
Elena Berriolo
Sylvia Beverly
Deepa Bhalerao
Ulrich Birkmaier
Richard Blanco
Alison Blunt
Agnes Bookbinder
James D. Booker
Dianne Borsenik
Brenda Bowen

Phil Brachi
Marie Bradby
Malorye Branca
Marek Brieška
Nadia
   Bruce-Rawlings
Moez Bunkheila
Kent Burgess
Mary Byrne
Christopher Cadra
Carmen Calatayud
Jeffrey Calzaloia
Monica Campbell
Jude Camwell
Nina Canal
Norma Cantu
Santiago Carbajal
Lauren Carlson
Shira Z. Carmel
Antoine Cassar
Jorge Centofanti
Shannon
   Chakraborty
Peter Chaltas
Brian Chambers
Marija Chandler
Brian Chappell
Hayan Charara
Diane Chehab
Kimberly Compton
Kelly Conklin
Jean Conrad
Mary Jane Copps
John Crawford

Sanja Cvetkovska
Dima Dajani
David Dansky
Pat Davis
Martha deBarros
Matthew Del Nevo
Lori Desrosiers
Michael Dickel
Elan Divon
Peter Dixon
Sharon Dolin
Peter Duckett
Chris Duel
Anca Dumitrescu
Riham El Adl
Yehia El Gammal
Sally El Hosaini
Sherif El Hosseny
Tamer El-Leithy
Sherine Elbanhawy
Jeremy Elbert
Sumaya Ali Elkhider
   Ali
Kristin Ellefsen
Christopher Ellis
Mohamed Elsamahi
Mido Emad
Jamie Etheridge
Cathy Ewald
Ahmed Fahmy
Maged Fahmy
Maria-Olga Fahmy
Azzam Fakhreddin
Siobhan Fallon

Thomas Farber
Naila Farouky
Jeremy Fernando
BK Fischer
Richard Foerster
Richard Ford
Daniel Fraser
FraYS
Ani G.
Sherine Gamal
  El Dine
Kamil Gamal ElDin
Anu Garg
Joseph Gauss
Sally Giar
Maz Gilmour
Iddo Ginat
Robert Givich
Sukie Gladstone
James Goddard
Ken Gosse
Mark Goulden
Brandon Graham
Steven Gray
Maree Grego
Jeff Gross
Sanjay Gupta
Michael Haaren
Jocelin Hackathorn
Rachel Hadas
Pamela Haladjian
Jeremy Halinen
Joshua Halinen
Youssef Hammad

Shérine Hanafi
Stephen Hanchey
Shadab Hashmi
Tariq Haydar
Scarlett Headley
Judith HeartSong
Mohamed Hefzy
Cherine Helmy
Charlie Helps
Terry Henderson
Emunah Herzog
Dalia Hidayat
Mark Hiebert
Omar Hikal
Udo Hintze
Agneta Hirschman
H. L. Hix
Cindy Hochman
Frankie Holliday
Paul Hopper
Mitzi Humphrey
Stephen Huppert
Janice Hutchinson
Adel Ibrahim
Nadia Ibrashi
Nagy Iskander
William Jackson
Parissa Jahangiry
Afshan Jahania
Randa Jarrar
Stephanie Johnson
Wanda Collins
  Johnson
Lois P. Jones

Carla Jordan
Sheema Kalbasi
Glen Kalem
Max Kalhammer
Ahmed Kamel
Laura M Kaminski
  (Halima Ayuba)
Joanna Kane
Scott Kaufman
Kay
Ami Kaye
Kathleen Kendrick
Elzahraa Ellie Khadr
Diana Khalil
Dan Kieran
Alex King
Beth Kirkhart
Dina Kiszonak
Angela Kleis
Dana Kletter
Kathryn Kopple
Sunita Kripalani
Lorenzo Kristov
Asser Samir
  Lababidi
Nadim Lababidi
Omar Lababidi
Samir Lababidi
Sawsan
  Lababidi-Dajani
April Lawson
Karin P. Lease
Andréana Lefton
Linda Legters

231

Melina Lekkas
Beth Levin
Kris Lindbeck
Moses Ling
Jeanne Loganbill
James Lough
Ali Lubbad
Linda M
Leila Maani
Margaret
  Mackinnon
Ahmed Maher
Ramy Maher
Steven Maimes
Leah Maines
Jack Marsh
Lucy Marx
Clif Mason
Hala Matar
James Mauch
Kate Mcgeever
Brendan
  McLoughlin
Joseph McMahon
Lisa Mecham
Silva Merjanian
Athina Merkouris
LaVonne Meyer
Salem Mikdadi
Salwa Mikdadi
Julia Veble Mikić
Terry
  Minchow-Proffitt
Tracy Mishkin

John Mitchinson
Nada Mobarak
Sanjay Monie
Dina Montasser
Michele Moorehead
Belinda Mora
Christopher Morgan
Sherif Mortagy
Peter Mortimer
Atefeh Naeemi
Sammy Nakhla
Betty Napier
Rod Naquin
Marwan Nashar
Carlo Navato
Saliha Nazir
Tracy NC
Mary Nees
Marilyn R Nelson
Annie Nguyen
Matthew Nienow
Jehane Noujaim
Ľuboš Novotný
Banjo O'Feral
Zora ONeill
Jillian Parker
Michael Parker
Maxine Patroni
Paulr
Robin Pender
Harry Penders
Dan Peters
Sylvia Petter
Justin Pollard

Rebecca Porteous
Carla Power
Sanna Ra
Dominique Radanyi
Rema Rajeshwari
Asma Rama
Shaun Randol
Sunita Rappai
Michelle Reale
Anne Restrepo
Diana Restrepo
Edwina Restrepo
Lisa Sofia Restrepo
Patricia Restrepo
Suzanne Restrepo
Adrian Rice
Cat Richardson
Tarak Rindani
Rowena Hutchinson
  Ritchie
Elizabeth Roach
Leila Roberts
Wyn Roberts
Alex Valencia
  Rodallec
Vicci Rodgers
Gloria Rodikis
Mary Ann Rose
Rowayat
Lindsey Royce
Sarah Russell
Ahmed Sabry
Karen Salazar
Noha Saleh

Vicki Sands
Pamela Saraf
Vikas Saraf
Karin E Schmidt
Deborah
  Schoenholz
Robin Scofield
Kristen Scott
Tara Seabra
Mo Semary
Kitty Shafique
Dolly Shalaby
Soraya Shalforoosh
Matthew Shenoda
Mira Shihadeh
Zarin Shoaib
Michael Sierchio
Ian Singleton
Edith Catalina
  Juarez Siordia
Leslie Skoda
James Smith
Polly Smock
Nadin Soliman
John Spaulding
Quentin Spender
Rochelle Spiker
Alex Stein
Elizabeth Steiner

Arin Stevens
Eric K. Stevens
Katia Stevens
Gregory H. Strong
Jennifer Stuart
Dirk-Jan
  Swagerman
Lucinda Szebrat
Ibrahim Tahir
Susannah Tarbush
Barbara Taylor
Laura Taylor
Tiffany Taylor
Stevan Thomas
Jasper Thornton
Melekper Toussoun
Ryan Trushenski
Lena Tuffaha
Rob Twigger
Kalu U
Onder Uluyol
Kimberly Urrea
Pam Uschuk
Neeshad V. S
Lee van Laer
Marianne van
  Lochem
Rosa Metzli
  Villalobos

Yolande Villemaire
Arthur Vincie
Katherine von Alt
Chris Wade
Ranitta Wagdy
Amelia Walker
Joanne Wang
Russell Ward
Whitney J. Wells
Hannah Whelan
Gina Williams
Stan Wood
Felix Woods
Wendy Woolfork
Daniel Wuenschel
Tabatha Yeatts
Alexis York
Marly Youmans
Maged Zaher
Taya Zayadi
Jailan Zayan
Suzanne Zeidy
Jill Zimmerman
Gary Zmolek
翟彧 Zhai Yu Zöe
Lara Zureikat
Samer Zureikat